Of Magic and Madness

KV Thompson

DEDICATION

In memory of my giants that have fallen towards the sky.

CONTENTS

ACKNOWLEDGMENTS

To love.
To depression.
To children.
To stress.
To family.
To murder.
To happiness.
To friends.
To broken hearts.
To the spectrum.
To inspiration.

Thank you for the journey.

Magic of the Heart.

Cause the **love notes** I write.

I.

Sometimes

I listen to my heartbeat

and wish its rhythm

was dancing with yours.

II.

Some of it

is messy

and unkind.

He said

you cannot

love every

part.

I said

you cannot

have a

complete story

without

every page.

III.

I once loved a kindred spirit.

His soul melted

into mine.

IV.

He was mist.

I breathed and breathed and breathed

until I felt him

in my lungs.

V.

You can love

every spot of me.

Just remember

there is no need

to clean

the mess.

There are flaws.

VI.

He is a storm.

But I am

tomorrow.

It will clear.

VII.

I'm more

of a

mess

than they

say.

You tidied

and tended

and tired

your way

through it

all.

I thank you.

VIII.

I can't help

but wonder how

you made

your smile

reflect

my thought

of you.

IX.

I watch you

from every corner

of me.

You've turned

enough to

see me

notice.

X.

He said I shouldn't

fall in love

that easy.

I said

you shouldn't

think love

can help

itself.

XV.

I did not think

I could love

again

until I showed him

my scars

and he replied,

"I've never seen

a person

so whole."

XVI.

Love

is being

validated

for no other reason

than because

you exist.

XVII.

Bare

yourself

within me.

Don't worry.

Your seed

will be buried

in

water.

And flesh.

It will grow.

XVIII.

I swept within my

flesh

and touched

love

till

it spirited me

away.

XIX.

He loved me

where I was

told

it could not

reach.

Guess I'm not

made of

voids

like they

said.

XX.

Imagine

being in

love

so fiercely

and

so softly

you sweep away

till your end

of time.

XXI.

It's not

the curve

of your lip

or the slope

of your nose.

I see the beauty in that.

But the way

you

tighten your grip

in every clutch

that makes me

see why

I've noticed those

things.

You're beautiful.

From the **lessons** I learn.

I.

I didn't want to be

bare.

I wanted to be

clothed in

all the words

they say about me.

Till their words

burned away

and I had

nothing left

to dress myself with

but

the words

and me.

II.

Find yours.

She happened.

Like we all do.

I happened.

And you're still

looking

cause sometimes

we happen

and are found

and put back.

We realize

we're still searching

and can't bring on the

journey

what someone else

might be

looking for.

III.

I wished

for him

and made him be

what I

wished for

but

you can't change

people

that were wished

for by

someone else.

You find yours.

IV.

They say Black

Woman

large

she fill a room like smoke

so no one can

breathe.

I say Black

Woman

spread so much

she made to air

for your lungs

and set you

free.

V.

Cry.

Show me

you have feeling

in there

where they say

men have only

voids.

VI.

I don't know if I should

love him

but I know

I've been loved

and that's the

reason why

I'm here.

So maybe I should

show him a reason

too.

VII.

You think

I'm trying to

fill myself with

you.

They never told

you can't fill

what is not

empty.

VIII.

My heart

used to chase you

whenever I saw

your name on

my phone.

Now it just

waves hello

to its old

prey.

IX.

My heart

no longer skips

when I hear your name.

Now it likes to

walk a

different way.

X.

In life,

You born.

You grow.

You hurt.

You lesson.

You determine and try.

You stretch more.

You fall.

You sink.

You drown and learn to swim.

You surface and solitude.

And grow more.

And smile cause you know

the why.

XI.

I'll be

here.

I always have.

XII.

I can hear it.

It sounds

like

birth.

I knew I was going

to be here

again.

XIII.

I call

God

and I

respond.

XIV.

I learned

pain

and I know

loss

and I've seen

death

but I know

God

and I know

the way.

XV.

I wanted him

to save me

cause

I was drowning

and forgot

long ago

I learned

how to

swim.

Now I think

he's my savior

cause he held me

above water

when I could've

kicked myself

to shore

all along.

XVI.

I think

I miss love

like you miss

the moment

you turn child

to adult

and it just

happens

and you don't realize

you're growing

or loving

till you're looking back.

XVII.

Inspiration is watching

a bird struggle to create its nest

and realizing there's something

beautiful there.

XVIII.

Building

is dressing your

inside with

every softness

ever spoken

to you.

XIX.

Creating

is circling

around yourself

until you've

wrapped and stitched and cursed

and dived.

And drowned.

And birthed.

And lived.

XX.

In the quest

to figure out

who I am,

sometimes

I forget

I've been here

before.

XXI.

It all

ends

in the

middle.

You've been

here before

and you'll

come

back

again.

XXII.

I can't go back

to where we

were birthed

but my home

has decided

to live

in me.

XXIII.

The darkness

decided to

consume me

one night.

I had to

show it

that

I am

light.

XXIV.

I'm here.

A spoken word.

A mother's cry.

A trying soul.

And there has to be

some beauty

in that.

XXV.

And when the walls

come toward me.

Telling all of

my secrets.

There. Still.

Was no achievement

greater than

me leaving.

XXVI.

I see her

in all

that is beautiful

and lost.

She will find

her way

when she

sheds

the lie.

XXVII.

I dressed myself

hoping

they wouldn't

see where

I've been.

I'll never

wear that

lie again.

XXVIII.

I told him

I found happiness.

He replied,

where?

I cried,

right here,

right here,

right here.

XXIX.

A tenderness.

A softer word.

A lighter grasp.

Will fill me more

deeply.

More

wholly

than

sharing a piece

of me.

XXX.

I

appreciate

the spectrum.

It covers

me whole

without needing

to choose

sides.

XXXI.

It's ok

to hurt.

You feel

and suffer

as much as

you feel

and smile.

It's ok

to happy.

And I **heal**, somehow.

I.

My heart races

and aches

and squeezes till

my eyes well

and then it feels

and fills

and you can't squeeze it or

it'll spill.

II.

Girl

you enuff.

That dark

and light

stretch marked

ass

and thigh.

That sometimes

hairy

and high

sometimes

waxed bald.

That scar.

Those scars.

You enuff.

Those dents

in your legs.

The jello

that waves

hello

when you walk.

Girl, you enuff.

All of you.

All that in you.

All that about you.

Girl,

you enuff.

And

you deserve

Love.

III.

I am worlds.

I move and control and create.

I damage and make better.

I try and try

again.

IV.

I've listened to

waves

and heard

thunder

on some days

and

gentleness

on others

and I wonder if

they noticed

they can hear

my cries if they just

listened to the

ocean.

V.

It's easy

because

I can see it

prodding and pulling me

open.

And I don't want to close it.

No.

I need to share.

VI.

I hid.

And shrunk

myself

until

I could

not fill myself

or till I could

fit in myself

too many

times.

And because

I've made so much

room inside

myself

I can finally

see what's

broken.

VII.

I wanted to be

beautiful.

I starved myself

in the

mirror.

I studied myself

in the

gathering.

And it all

came back

to me

in a wonder

and no wonder

I didn't see before

cause I wouldn't

look

right here.

In here.

VIII.

I've cried

with my eyes

wide open

and I've been

killed

and broken

and beaten

and I just

won't

die

cause my soul stays alive.

IX.

Let me

walk this

path

till my soles

run smooth.

I'll walk

this path

even after.

X.

I saw

my future

in a dream.

It told me

don't tell.

Don't speak.

Unfold the story

before it

sinks.

XI.

Who are

you

to tell me

I can't love

here?

Then told

me to leave.

That's why

I got to

come back.

I'll love.

XII.

You aren't a

ruin.

Those are

forgotten and forebode.

Yes, you are

old

but

you're a story

that will always be

told.

XIII.

I'm not

alone.

I'm here.

Sometimes

that's more

than enough.

XIV.

I saw my

yesterday

and realized

it watches me

too.

XV.

My mother

was born

and shattered

and crossed

and coated

and cleaned

and cleansed

and back again.

And she's here.

And she's whole.

And she birthed.

XVI.

My father

cried and

fought and

listened and

feared and

loved and said

he wouldn't and

he held his

daughter

and said

he

must.

XVII.

Word art.

I am word art.

XVIII.

I don't know

how the air

can kiss me

and whisk me

away

and smother me

all in one

sweep.

But I know

the air is

sweet

and can

warm me

till I

sleep.

XIX.

I haven't

lived in a

sure way.

But I've lived

and tried

and cried

and stretched till my

blood flowed

and my heart

groaned.

And I've sure

lived some

way.

XX.

We are fragile

like the

softest

breath in

new air.

XXI.

Maybe if you see

how tainted

I am

or how beautiful

I am

or how twisted

I am

or how unashamedly me

I am

you would understand

how I'm made of

both

magic and

madness.

XXII.

I'm spread

like sand

in the ocean.

Torn to pieces

but soft

to the touch.

XXIII.

Speak

until your sound

resonates

with the

walls.

XXIV.

I've lived.

I live.

I'll live.

XXV.

Who are we

but the feet

of our ancestors?

XXVI.

Who am I

but the love story

of my parents?

XXVII.

What is perfect

but love

gotten

carried away?

XXVIII.

What is love

but realizing

you feel it

too?

XXIX.

Remember

who you were

before they

told you

it would hurt?

Find her

and tell her

she can

heal.

XXX.

I built my

home

in me

so it can

travel

(cause I'm

free!)

Madness in the Mind.

From what they teach us
growing up here.

I.

Bang, bang.

Kill.

That's how we deal.

II.

Black child sing

with your spirit so free.

What will you croon

when there is no me?

Brown child soar

with your spirit so high.

What will you lift

when the teacher has died?

Red child speak

with your spirit so right.

What will you say

when I can no longer fight?

Colored child

please keep your spirit aligned.

What will you do

when they come to silence your mind?

III.

Today in class

a white girl said her

dad always told her to

never drive down the

state streets at night.

I live on Utah.

IV.

Black Black Black

girl

with Black Black

skin.

White White White

world

For White White

men.

Try try try

girl

to win win win.

Wear that mask

girl.

Hold that

grin.

V.

I fight my

tears

in hopes

that

if I don't

cry

time will

stop

passing.

VI.

I didn't tell my dad

he touched me.

I thought he would kill him.

That greasy old man with his

brownish fingernails

and smoldering smell.

I didn't tell my dad

he tried to touch me

with those hands.

Sliding, slick like, to

my prepubescent thigh.

Caressing. Stroking. Touching.

With those dirty fingernails.

I didn't tell my dad

he tried to unzip my pants

with those hands.

Grabbing my tiny zipper.
I remember tasting my heartbeat
as he got it half way down.

I didn't tell my dad
he tried to touch me.
I just coughed,
and saved that dirty fingernail
man's life.

VII.

I gave you

the

love

I couldn't give myself

and wondered why

I always felt

empty.

I needed that.

VIII.

I left him

and

he asked,

"I hurt you?"

On the same

tongue

he cut me

with.

IX.

And my

baby died.

And I didn't think

anything

worse could

happen.

And worse

could happen.

You just

have to

wait for it.

X.

We didn't hear

a heartbeat

the last time.

Now I hear

mine too

loudly.

Too rapid.

Too much.

I wonder if

she left hers

inside of

me

when I

birthed her.

XI.

I lost my mind.

No one noticed.

I smiled

and laughed

and danced

and talked the same

and walked the same

and my mind went on journeys

of a past I can't remember

and a trauma and a memory

and I missed my favorite show

and I lost my favorite socks

and I haven't cooked in months

and I sleep with the lights on

and I've lost my mind

and I'm normal

and I'm hurt

and I'm the same

and I'm insane

and I can't remember you

and him and her and numbers

and faces and places and

histories.

And I can't remember.

And I work.

And I go.

And I travel.

And I put together.

I look put together.

And I've lost it.

And I'm lost.

And I've lost.

I'm a loss.

And no one noticed.

XII.

I'm more than

a mask.

A veil.

A screen.

But he

closed my doors

and said it's too

much in here.

Too much.

XIII.

I took my

scars

and showed them

to an onlooker.

They

bled the wounds

again.

XIV.

He stretched me

till I was made

smooth

and softened.

But now

I'm spread

wide

and they've all come

to feel

what I'm

made of.

XV.

I can have

a heart

made of silk

and satin

and still be told

I shouldn't have

happened.

The **conversations** we have.

I.

I imagine my death

every night

and they

say

you can't come yet.

You can't come yet.

You have to

get it right.

II.

Peak into

me. Speak into

me. Let your

voice remind.

Lay upon

me. Say upon

me. Creep into

my mind.

III.

Come visit me

when the sun

turns us

over to the

night.

IV.

Do you care

to taste my tears?

Flavors of

my hopes

and fears.

V.

Would you mind

if I were dead?

A ghost

that lives

within

your head.

VI.

Why do you

fill me up

to let me down?

Do you like

the way I smile?

I love you here.

I love you now.

But you can't seem

to stay around.

VII.

You can live

in me

if you don't

seek to please

what's there.

VIII.

This is

all of me.

I hope you don't

go searching

for more.

IX.

There is more.

I just haven't

found it

yet.

X.

I want to be whole again.

Like every piece

I've ever shared

placed back

in the shape

of me.

XI.

Maybe I'll

try again

when the rain

becomes a bathing warm

and not

a spring storm.

XII.

I wish

souls told

the story of yesterday.

Maybe I wouldn't

be trying this

again.

XIII.

I told myself

in order to heal

I need to pour

myself

into the earth

until

I return to

dust and

sand.

XIV.

I once told my mama

I wanted to cut my hair.

You know what she told me?

"Beauty is for those

who can withstand pain."

I thought she was calling me ugly

but,

that's neither here nor there

so I felt no shame.

I just chopped

and watched

my strands

brush past my chair

and wondered if beauty

had any beauty to share?

XV.

The world could end

and if I lived

and you were with me too,

I'd probably send my soul

to Him

so I wouldn't be with you.

You showed me pain

and opened wounds

I should've never knew.

So I'd rather spend my life

in fire

than living it with you.

And **questions** we ask ourselves.

I.

Where were

you

when I ached

more than I ever have?

You said you loved

so big

you can feel my hurt.

You're still alive,

so did you really

love me?

II.

What do you do

when you

grow

but never

learned

the lesson?

Is that the moment

we

return?

III.

I wonder

if I can find

my peace

in a

piece.

IV.

Are there more places to visit?

Somewhere bigger

than what's

inside of me?

V.

Why can't I see

in me

the world

that sees in me?

VI.

What is life

but coming

again?

VII.

What is forever

but my presence

found

in the archives?

VIII.

Is

nowhere free

for a black girl

like

me?

IX.

Sometimes

I listen to

my heartbeat

and ask it

"why

do you keep beating

although you

can no longer

feel?"

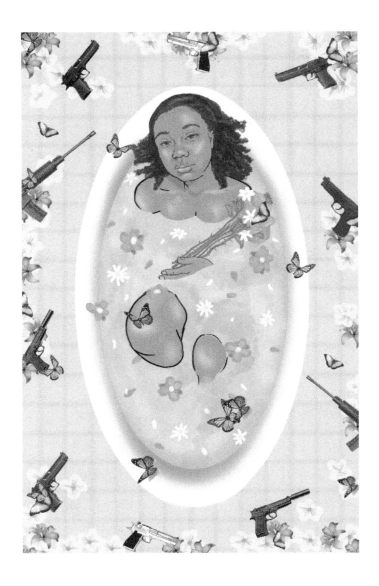

About the Author.

KV Thompson is a magical black girl born and raised in St. Louis, MO. She's still there. Surrounded by guns and geraniums, and still managing to make a way.

Made in the USA
Monee, IL
01 November 2021